STEP
IN
THE
BOAT

a lifelong journey of purpose

by
J. Scott Spector

Step in the Boat
a lifelong journey of purpose
by
J. Scott Spector

First edition by JScott Partners Publishing Division, JScott Partners, Inc., Birmingham, AL

JScott Partners Publishing
130 Inverness Plaza, Suite 380
Birmingham, AL 35242
www.brookestoneassociates.com

Book design: Joel Friedlander
Printed in the United States of America

ISBN 978-1-0703-0036-8

Dedication

Thank you to my birth mother for going through with it, without you, none of this life is possible. Thank you to my mother and dad who raised, loved and cared for me through their own imperfections. Thank you to my many friends who encouraged me to share the journey. I thank my son, Logan and daughter, Marissa, who without their continued love, encouragement and support, I would not have found my true calling in life.

Contents

Epilogue

Preface

I've avoided writing a 'how it all began piece' for several years, as what I do is not about me; frankly, no one would care or be interested in reading 'the story'. However, the feedback from people I care about and value their input changed my perspective. My deepest thanks go to my dear friends – the people who encouraged me to get it out of my head and on paper. This book is from my heart.

If you're wondering, I'm not revealing some secret vulnerability nor am I afraid to share 'what's underneath' because there is no mask, and there is nowhere to hide. After posting on my blog, *The Culture Whisperer*, for several years, writing a book, numerous speaking gigs, coaching hundreds of executives, business professionals and countless consulting projects, I thought there was enough 'history' shared where most of you would 'get it'. Even if people were remotely interested on where I came from, why I am the way I am and what happened along the way, you'd figure it out on your own. Resisting the unveiling wasn't about being stubborn or fearing any negative reaction, I figured it would bore most of you...you asked, here it is.

What I tell you in the dark, speak in the daylight; what is whispered in your ear, proclaim from the roofs. – Matthew 10:27 NIV

CHAPTER 1

It's Now or Never

It was nearly sixty years ago when two crazy college kids met at a typical party in the Fan District of Richmond, Virginia adjacent to Richmond Polytechnic Institute, what is now Virginia Commonwealth University. A girl from a blue-collar family in southwestern Virginia and the son of an ambassador from a tiny middle eastern country met. Today, you'd call it 'they hooked up.' My guess is they danced to the Elvis Pressley tune. I am the product of that 'hookup' and here's where you can make the assumption, I've made countless times over.

On one hand, I can say they were two star-crossed lovers who unexpectedly had a child out of wedlock. On the other, I can say, I'm the product of a college party gone horribly wrong.

Our perspective shapes our reality. I can choose to go from one extreme to another. It is the theme of my life over those six decades. Much has changed since that time, and all I know about my biological parents comes from what wasn't redacted in the adoptive paperwork I acquired years ago.

I respect my birth mother's decision, and, in that respect, I've chosen not to search. There's no desire to find her at this stage of life. However, from a medical history perspective, it would've been nice to know what's unknown. Then again, does it really matter?

When I'm asked to speak, I always give thanks to my mother, 'for going through with it'; for in today's society, I may not exist if many people had it their way – cross it off their list in life as if 'it' never existed – I never existed. I'm deeply thankful for the women out there who for a variety of reasons, CHOOSE to go through with it – have a baby and give life to a family who cannot. If it wasn't for that decision, none of what I'm about to share happens.

At six weeks, my adopted family took me home and cared for me as if I was their very own natural child. Of course, it was a loving home and I felt special every day. Life is a gift and I'm living proof of that gift.

My dad was an outdoor advertising sales manager working for Ed Turner, founder and owner of Turner Advertising. The billboards dotted the eastern seaboard of I-95 from New York to Miami in the late fifties and early sixties.

Ed Turner, the father of Ted Turner, the -to be media mogul many of us know today. Ted cut his teeth under dad's guidance for many years. My mother was a switchboard operator and occasional pageant girl when not partying at the beach.

When I was old enough to understand story time, my mother would read a series of books by Florence Rondell and Ruth Michaels, *The Adopted Family* and *The Family That Grew*, on how special an adopted child is imprinting on me I wasn't an accident; that I wasn't the bastard child I was born. I always enjoyed listening to mother read while I sat in her lap. I am grateful for the gift of life.

My early years seemed like any suburban child's life, oblivious to my surroundings in the 60's playing outside in the yard or with Lady, our 8-year old beagle. I was new and different, and I smelled funny to her. Growing up in a typical southern rambler with a neighborhood of dozens of kids – some of which I'm still friends with thanks to the good side of social media.

I remember summertime on Baysdale Lane was always special as we'd block off the street, and all the families would cookout together. We'd play flashlight tag and kick the can and chase each other with sparklers or catch lightning bugs in glass jars.

As the years went by and friends slowly moved away to other neighborhoods, cities or towns, distance became common. We would see each other during school or at the pool or baseball games during the summer months. Our time together became less and less unfortunately. Something else, rather dark happened which would begin to shape and mold my inexperience.

Like most children, I had two sets of grandparents who were wonderful to me accepting me as one of their own. During the summer after completing first grade, I learned the meaning of death or at least what a six-year old can comprehend. For each of the next three summers, a grandparent passed away and I'd come to equate summer with death – seems logical.

So much so, my last day of school in 4th grade, I asked mother 'when will granny die this summer'. Thankfully, she ignored the childish remark and moved about her day. She died just before school started back that summer.

As my world began to open around me, another realization occurred becoming more aware of people and things. I've learned over the years; children gain a heightened sense of awareness around the ages of 10-12 especially between their parents. My world began to expand rather quickly outside of my little bubble. I'm sure it occurs with some children sooner or later, but in my experience coaching sports to that age group for over ten years it's a very critical age.

Kids either tend to become resilient and adapt well or they begin to withdraw and struggle. Unfortunately, the emotional choices their little minds make can shape and change their perspective on life as they know it. It dramatically shapes children favorably or unfavorably given their own unique set of circumstances.

For me, I noticed a change in both of my parents I'd never realized until now; a sense of stress, strife and an uneasy climate in our home. Their personalities began to change, or my awareness increased or both. I knew something was different in how they were, how they acted – their behavior. I had no idea what it was until our last trip to Virginia Beach as a family in '72. As long as I could remember, we'd always spend two to three weeks at a cottage on 53rd Street steps from the ocean. But this year, we were miles away and to me we might as well have been hours away.

This trip taught me what danger looked like and what the word 'drunk' means – it scared me. That week, all innocence was lost. That week taught me life as I knew it would no longer be the same. I had to grow up and learn the silver-spoon I was born into would be traded for a plastic fork and a fifth of Smirnoff.

We returned to Richmond, began to pack all our things into boxes and move away from the friends I'd grown up with and to a different neighborhood.

I didn't understand and didn't know how to react or respond, because this was a new experience for me. What I did know and cling to was sports – football, baseball and basketball. It was one of a few constants in my life growing up. All of us on our block played ball and we all had fun playing together. Even though I grew up during the civil rights era, I was raised as we're all one big family of immigrants. My adopted parents were Russian Jews and Scottish-Irish and I previously mentioned my biological father was from the Middle East.

We'd had a maid for as long as I can remember and picking up Willie Mae was always a highlight of the week for me. I never saw color in her nor her two sons, Boochie and Darryl, whom I called my brothers.

I didn't care we looked different. We played ball together, read and colored books and did everything together for many years. As that final summer with Willie Mae passed, my parents told me I'm to be bussed across town to another school away from my friends. At least no one died that year.

Instead of going to Thomas Jefferson in the heart of Richmond, they decided to enroll me in private school; another group of friends I'm still connected to thanks to social media. Because of my own internal struggle with my parents (that I had no consciousness of), I went to two different private schools before settling into Steward School. Apparently, I was unable to get along with the authority of 'the penguins' – the parochial kids will understand.

Quick story: I'd had about enough from Sister Mary Margaret. She didn't like me because I started in her classroom three months after school began. The late start occurred after an unfortunate incident at my first parochial school, which we don't need to chase the rabbit down that hole.

I was an interruption to Sister Mary and her crusty aura. My fondest memory of her, however, was my last day there when after she'd pulled my ear and whacked me on my head with a ruler.

With respect I said, 'penguin, hit me one more time with that ruler and it's on.' I excused myself and walked to the Headmaster's office so he could call my parents...again.

My parents were known to have a cocktail or two especially at the beach. Hey, we're on vacation! I get it. But, the next three years of my parent's drinking became worse and worse. I didn't understand the why of it all. I just knew something was different again. The arguing and fighting began, dishes and glasses breaking which seemed like nightly events. I remember making an off-hand comment, 'if y'all keep throwing stuff, we won't have anything left to eat off of.' I learned how to duck flying Spode and Wedgewood fairly well as I was pretty good at dodgeball in school.

Apparently, there may have been a pattern with me speaking my mind. They took turns passing out on the couch. All I could do was bury myself in sports and school. I didn't realize it at the time, but those were my escapes and how I kept myself grounded and not succumbing to the worst.

I'm now the typical child of alcoholic parents, always overachieving; not knowing what any of that meant then. It wasn't until my forties when I realized this was my cry for help. The wound of rejection had finally found a home.

This story is not to make you feel sorry for me whatsoever, and I don't want your pity nor your sympathy. Teenagers have a lot of feelings rolling around inside. I felt rejected by my biological parents and am living with rejection from my adopted parents. No one wants me around. Why else would they do that to themselves?

I can see where some of you would call me selfish. I can see where some of you may empathize with my situation. I was too young to understand it was their own demons they're wrestling with, but I'm naive enough to heap the burden on my back as unloved and unwanted. I couldn't get through the next four years fast enough. Please Lord, let me turn the page and start my life over. I don't belong here. I'm not wanted. I didn't ask for this!

CHAPTER 2

Last Call

Mother moved out as I began sophomore year and I returned to public school because we couldn't afford private school anymore. She left dad and I alone to sober up and recover. Moving in with her sister in Lynchburg, she was able to turn her life around and start anew. She'd heard her last call. I knew if she could start over, then so could I. I saw a ray of hope for myself if I can make it that far.

The first three months of my sophomore year are pretty much a blur maybe because I've blocked most of those memories out of my mind. What I do remember is leaving for school in the morning, dad asleep in his chair and finding him in the same position six or eight hours later.

By this time, I'd given up a promising baseball career because I was too embarrassed to ask for rides to practices and games. I had to keep up the appearance I had it together, when, in fact, mother was gone, and dad was always hammered.

This isn't a normal life, and certainly not one any child should live through. He hadn't worked for almost three years and we were living off savings and the inheritance from his father's estate. I learned how to cook, clean and do laundry by myself. Mother rarely called and I didn't really care to hear from her either. In my eyes, she quit. As I matured and became a parent, I understood she saved herself although at a pretty high cost. There was no forgiveness yet.

By the time the holiday break rolled around, I called mother and told her I can't do this anymore and to come get me. My last memory with dad was spending Christmas there with him. It was just he and I alone in the dark listening to Johnny Mathis' Christmas Album.

I'd put the tree up after Thanksgiving, because that's what we always did. I was trying to recreate as much sameness I could muster in my newfound dysfunction. I remember sitting there in the dark watching the tree while he lay motionless in his chair. Mother would not come get me immediately after I called. Her behaviors were often strange to me and I never received a reason.

I waited until she showed up the day after New Year's to move 120 miles southwest from what I knew was home. We didn't start school until the following Monday, but I always thought it odd of her to wait two weeks to get me.

I moved to a city I didn't want to be in, to a school I didn't want to go to with people I didn't want to get to know. I would tell myself, 'if I can just survive for a couple more years, I can make it on my own away from all this noise.' I didn't want to move away from dad as it meant I'm admitting defeat and I was unsure if she was clean enough to live with. I was still angry at her for leaving. I did know I had to let my dad go if I was to survive.

Fifty-four days later, on Friday the 13th, my dad died due to an accident in the house. It was a gruesome sight. A 15-year old doesn't need to see blood trails in a home they once lived in. Guilt flooded over me. Seeing my old home in disarray with blood-soaked carpets, splattered handprints everywhere and an odd scent I still can't get out of my nose made me angry and hurt.

I could have saved him. It was my fault. I've lost my dad the only person who loved me. According to the autopsy, when he fell backwards onto the brick steps, he cut an artery in his neck and bled out. Another wound opens inside me.

One of my fondest memories, before alcohol dominated his life, was our Saturday's. For what seemed to me like every Saturday, dad and I would drive to the Jefferson Hotel for a haircut. It was a beautifully wood paneled and marbled floor space on a lower floor of the historic hotel, and it smelled of Clubman and Vitalis.

I'd sit there quietly while dad got his haircut and listen to the older guys tell college stories and share political opinions. After the weekly trim, we'd go to the Azalea Garden and feed the ducks at Bryan Park. During the spring we'd walk through the beautiful array of flowers there.

There was a beautiful display of red and white azaleas in the shape of a cross about the size of a football field. In the fall, I remember the changing colors of the leaves and the chill in the air. When I was little, he'd carry me on his shoulders and introduce me to friends or passersby as 'the Chairman of the Board.' Sometimes, we'd take in a Richmond Spiders football game at City Stadium where he graduated in '52.

I realize we didn't go every weekend, but my memory painted very vivid pictures of our time together. On our way home, we'd stop by the bakery on Broad Street to pick up pastries and fresh bread.

It was a very special time for us, for me. I can't recall a single conversation, but the images are still as bright today as they were then. I moved my own family from Atlanta to Birmingham in the summer of 2002. I'd recreate those images as much for me as it was for my son, Logan, where we'd go to Edgar's at the Colonnade for pastries and treats.

A day doesn't go by where I don't think about dad, our memories, and all of the 'first's' of life he'd never be a part of. I was blessed last year reading *Wild at Heart* after it being recommended by a friend. If you've ever read any of John Eldredge's works, you'll understand.

My dad was far from perfect, but he was my dad and our good times together are still cherished. I made damn sure my children's lives would be cherished times as well. I'm not leaving this world without them knowing everyday they're loved, and their dad is committed to them every single day regardless any circumstances.

We all face a journey, an adventure. What I've come to learn is ALL of us have had devastating things happen in our lives – most of which will never leave our lips sadly. My hope is your lessons and your blessings give you the courage to keep going. Every one of you has a story, and it should be told if you have the courage to share it.

I've also learned is time helps you through your own healing process. Part of that process is to tell your story also. If you are to find freedom in your life and eventually move forward, it must come out along with all the feelings, good and bad, one last time.

My reason for putting it on paper is a hope no one faces a road like this one and to allow God's healing powers to comfort, strengthen and encourage me - perhaps you, too. It's been said, you're either going into a storm, living in the storm or coming out of the storm. Again, a change of perspective.

With all the crap surrounding my life, I was very fortunate to be gifted with tremendous athletic ability. Anything with a ball, any sport, I excelled at and was recognized as such. I mostly played team sports until moving to southwest Virginia taking up golf – a sport my father played. I never saw him play although I have photos of him with several trophies. He never saw me play either.

I thrust myself into the sport escaping into that world every day. I played and hit balls from sunrise to sunset and beyond regardless of the weather. Mother would drop me off on her way to work and pick me up when she was done. It was as much therapy for me as it was honing a skill. I was determined to play the sport professionally.

Eventually, I found myself learning how to play at a daily-fee course in Forest, VA and one guy I'll never forget is Hilton Phillips. Hilton shaped my golf career one Friday afternoon after I asked him what it takes for me to play golf in college. He walked me to the cart barn, strapped on an empty trash can to the back of the cart and said, 'go fill this trash can with balls and hit every one of them every day for a year.'

He then threw the challenge out. 'Will you do it?' Without missing a beat, I said, 'yes.' A year later through days of rain, snow and sunshine, I went from shooting in the 80's to breaking par half the time. I had found a way out of my hell!

As I progressed, he made a few calls and entered me into several tournaments throughout the southeast. Several colleges were calling and before the Holiday's rolled around in '76, I'd traveled to Stillwater, Denton, San Diego, Columbia, Gainesville and Statesboro to see what college life looked like.

And by the following summer, I'd take my final visits before deciding on Georgia Southern, the same school Hilton graduated from along with several friends I'd made playing golf over the summers.

We didn't have AP classes back then, but I CLEP'd much of my freshman year and was very fortunate my grandfather had set up a trust fund to cover my education costs.

That fact made me an attractive addition to the college coaches who took the time to meet with me as I didn't cost them a scholarship. Born and raised in Virginia, yet not a single Virginia school even considered inquiring of my interest to attend their school. Don't think it didn't cross my mind that not even colleges here where I grew up wanted me. I want out!

I loved my trip to San Diego and didn't want to return home to Virginia. I was determined to move as far away from my mother as possible without being too far, and the west coast was just too far for my own comfort. What came out of that trip was a lifelong friend to this day.

I didn't have anywhere near the relationship with mother as I had with my dad, but I couldn't leave her entirely. When August rolled around, I found myself playing beside Mike Donald, Jodie Mudd and Pat Lynn – all three who were All-American's during my tenure at Georgia Southern.

School was an adjustment as it is for nearly every college-age kid. I was very determined and very independent to live and to thrive. I also learned how to eat on $5 a week. I ate, slept and breathed golf. I was convicted to become a professional golfer, and I knew deep down I would make it.

I was very fortunate to make friends with these guys as we had some common ground and a common goal. During my time at Southern, we played some great courses around the US and finished in the top 10 both years nationally. My greatest thrill was to play Augusta National the week after the Masters – something I'll never forget. While walking the course, I immediately remembered the days with my dad in Bryan Park. It was like he was there at Augusta walking with me. Even when I've gone back, I can still smell the azaleas and magnolias as if I was there for the first time.

The next two years flew by and gave me enough courage and confidence to try my hand at the Tour. At the time, the mini-tours consisted of a handful of guys who hadn't made the grueling Q-school in the fall and the snowbird Club pros who 'donated' to us so we could pay our rent and food for a month off them.

Never trust a skinny guy with a squint and a 1 iron I'd always say. In fact, my nickname was '1 iron' because I was the size of one. It certainly wasn't anything close to what the Web.com Tour is today as most of us were playing for more money during practice rounds than during the tournaments. It was a fun time, no responsibilities – I thought. It wasn't a serious job as the kids are taught today from a very early age.

I quickly learned I wasn't ready to play for a living. I was immature and my cockiness hid my fear of failure and success. It may have been to my advantage to stay at GSC with two more years of eligibility left, but I graduated early and moved on with life with no regrets. The next seven years had me behind the counter and on the lesson tee as a sweater'n shoe pro of the PGA working throughout the country. But by the time the third employer I worked for filed bankruptcy, I figured the door to my golf career should close.

I had no interest in being a rep or solely a teacher...again, pretty naive. Then again, I didn't have someone I felt I could trust to ask, 'what the hell am I going to do with my life'? The only advice I can recall is hearing Board Member after board member tell me how impressed they were with my career trajectory, the programs and service excellence I present, but...'Scott, we can't hire you because you're single!'

Our daughters and granddaughters are your age and we don't want any appearance of any inappropriate situations.' What is a task-oriented guy to do? Get married, of course. Shortly after checking 'stability' off the list, I'm searching for a career outside of golf something I thought I'd never have to do.

I'm beginning to see a pattern as the next seven years, walked me through several companies where I had a 'real job'. My peers and mentors told me I was good at seeing things they didn't, and that realization became a cornerstone of my career. I knew back then if I had to start my career over, or as they say now – reinvent yourself – I'd need more education.

I often heard 'you can be whatever you want to be in life if you put your mind to it'. I also heard the stings from the naysayers as well, 'the you'll never make it'. Well, I'll show all of you. Needless to say, the chip on my shoulder is quite large at this point in life. It seemed as if I always felt I had to prove something all the time.

Life is filled with up's, down's, glimpses from the mountaintop and longer than desirable time in the valley. But most of all, we spend a great amount of our lives in between those two 'places'. I was told I could not play professional sports. I did. I was told I could not transition from soft goods to consumer goods. I did. I was told I could not go from retail to manufacturing. I did. I was told I'd never succeed on my own. I have. With every one of the 'no's' I experienced, failure existed and was overcome. I knew I could excel just from sheer will and determination.

CHAPTER 3

Be Kind, Rewind

I never saw my golf career as a failure. I didn't heap the familiar pain of rejection on me. Maybe because it was my decision alone within my control and a passionate sport I truly loved. I also learned very slowly and very subtly; people will take what you do well for their advantage if you're not careful. I was brought up to trust people in authority and I did, perhaps too much.

I didn't expect leader after leader to take what I do, assume the credit and then toss me aside like a worn dish rag. I heard the sound of rejection again. It must be something I'm not doing, something I'm missing. What is it I'd wonder?

The first time it occurred, my wife and I were living in the DC area with our two young children, and I had an opportunity to join a multi-national organization. I was tabbed as a 'fixer', the turnaround resource who goes in and tightens up operations while increasing top line. We moved 2,000 miles away from family and friends. My first week was a precursor to what would foreshadow my career.

With MBA in hand I was given an opportunity. An opportunity means we want to send you someplace you don't want to go and do something you don't want to do. I was familiar with this 'movie reel' playing a similar role before. This company I was 'opportuned for' was in the midst of introducing new products in their manufacturing systems while merging with another like manufacturer. I'd seen this scenario before and now understood why I was here.

We were less than three months from 'birthing a baby' into the marketplace. On day three of my new career, I asked what I thought was a simple question. 'If my math is correct, we are introducing 84 new items in 4 wood specie and we have 32 stain choices and 5 paint offerings.

That's roughly over 10,000 variations, right? What's our manufacturing plan to deliver these new products on time and within spec?' You would have thought I was questioning the resurrection of Christ.

I simply figured they were a helluva lot smarter than me, surely, they've done this before, surely, they have a plan, right? They didn't! From that day forward, I was the proverbial salmon swimming upstream.

After a few months of our new 'sales prevention program', I was given the opportunity to fix this self-induced fiasco. I fixed it and even worked with three CEO's while I was there. I was instrumental in taking my division from a turnover of $28M to $92M while net grew from -8% to 15% EBITDA. I did it and with a lot of help! What did I get in return? Thanks, and good luck. What? You're kidding right? The turnaround was successful, but I'm no longer needed. There's the next arrow of rejection. It was years later I accepted that season as a success.

To me, the career target was the opportunity to get international exposure and take a division overseas. While being led to believe (the carrot to keep me going), it's a viable opportunity, I would later learn it was never up for discussion.

'You're too valuable at the operating unit level. Now that you've successfully completed this one, we have an opportunity for you in Detroit or Cleveland.' After dangling Europe under my nose, I'm left with Cleveland? You just sent my ass to South Dakota and now my prize is the armpit of Hell?

Thank you, but no. Months later, I would get an offer from a Canadian outfit to grow their US presence based in Atlanta and we did. Unfortunately, I did not realize until it was too late the family-run business was undercapitalized. All the new business we generated – like a hockey stick – couldn't be produced fast enough to keep up with the steep growth. After seven months of my checks arriving late and later, I couldn't jeopardize my credibility by staying under these circumstances. Another lesson learned. Back to square zero, again. It was during this season my mother became very ill and was on a hospital-to-elder-care-to-emergency-room and back again rotation which lasted almost a year.

She'd had multiple surgeries for Sirois, couple heart cath's and several recurring tumors for a number of years. She even exclaimed one night in her morphine-induced stupor; the doctor's had relocated her belly button after her final heart surgery.

I would drive back-and-forth from Atlanta to Virginia multiple times a week based on the medical doctor's phone calls I'd routinely get usually between the hours of 1 and 3 am. Most of the times I would visit, she didn't recognize me or would call me dad's name. I came to the realization at forty-one this was no way to live and they're only practicing medicine. They don't know what's wrong with her. It wasn't prolonging life. It was extending death.

My children were very young and don't remember much about granny other than she was always sick, smoking or both. It was a blessing mother only suffered eight months before passing in her sleep.

While in Atlanta, my next home improvement iteration came with the opportunity to create and sell the next best mousetrap, or so I thought. The Sink-in-All, a do it yourselfer's dream in a box. One of the easiest weekend projects for a DIY consumer was to replace their sink. Through several relationships made over a handful of years, we birthed our own product importing it from overseas through a company who specialized in steel stamping products. We jumped into bed with the big orange box, tested it in Atlanta and sold out our first container in a little more than a week. Within three months, we were the hottest SKU going and I thought finally I won't have to struggle any more. My ship has come in, literally!

My ego got a well needed boost. Whatever goes up must come down, and we came down with a thud and a bump. It couldn't have gone much better or much worse but what a learning and an expensive experience.

Several more evolutions in the home improvement industry found me working for several companies in helping them figure out what's working, what's not and how to fill in the gaps.

It took a terrible strain on my personal life. I kept the kids as oblivious as possible to our marital situation, but kids are smart, and they got a sense of something's not quite right – just like I did at that age. I became a statistic and started life over again as a single parent.

The best thing I had going for me was the business relationships I'd made along the way. One of those relationships led me to join an Executive Search firm as all of the work I'd engaged in involves people. Regardless of raw materials, process, costs and profit, it's all about the people and somehow, we've slid off track for far too long.

We sacrifice people to make the bottom line look better. Hell, I was living proof of that! I began to research more and more about business process, lean manufacturing and made a great connection through a friend to the CEO of Allied Signal who would mentor me.

It took several – if anyone's counting, five - executives treating my skill set as disposable for me to say enough. Once they all took what they wanted from me, there was no need for me to be around. 'Uncle Larry', as I'd call my mentor, taught me how to keep my emotions in check and analyze situations from a variety of perspectives I'd not previously learned or experienced.

I learned more from him in one hour than I learned earning those three letters after my name. Slowly, I began to consider...if I'm to avoid repeating this situation again, then I have two choices – select better company's and leaders or go out on my own. What I lived through and learned was priceless.

We've all been there at some point in our life – married, children, mortgage, cars, debt, etc., can I or can I not afford to make the jump – to risk what I've worked so hard for to this point. In my case, I was down to my last $4 and realized I had nothing to lose.

It simply can't get any worse than it is now. I'm slowly beginning to understand my own success has been nothing more than a culmination of many failures and never giving up. Although I took each failure very personally, I don't want to see anyone get taken advantage of given their unique skills they bring to their employer.

My greatest takeaway and the initial reason I'm so passionate about leadership is I don't want anyone to work for someone who acknowledges their worth when it's in the company's favor and then become thrown away as if they were never born. I'd rather be treated like an old VHS movie rental – be kind and rewind. It stirs up the familiar feelings of dread typing these all too familiar sounds of rejection and abandonment.

CHAPTER 4

Discovering the Process

I began studying companies and executives from my earliest day through today to learn why and how highly successful executives failed and some with less talent succeed; what's the best profile to train someone up to a level of sustainable success and what's missing today in leadership.

In today's microwave society, we have hundred-fold more information at our fingertips in a millisecond than ever. With social media at its apex, everyone calls themselves an expert as throngs flock to like sheep to get a glimpse of greatness.

What few of these gurus advocate is there's a specific process and a specific order to follow to become a great leader. The process cannot be shortened. It cannot be circumvented, IF it – your leadership – is to last. You first must learn how-to lead yourself - that alone can take a lifetime. Next, is to lead another, then lead a small group of people, then a larger group. In time, you learn to lead a small company, then a larger one and finally a larger business or an organization. The model so many of us have grown up with is broken and it must stop!

Forty-plus years ago we RIF'd people to make the numbers and in many instances that mindset continues to perpetuate hundreds of organizations today. I decided to find or perhaps uncover a new model, a new process, of leadership.

I was always a notetaker for as long as I can remember. The more research I did, the more notes I'd take, filling notebook after notebook on good things and bad things that occur in businesses large and small, domestic and foreign. I began writing a blog as a means of getting my thoughts out of my head, away from the notebooks and onto the interweb. I remember back in my junior year of high school, being berated by my English Comp teacher that I may have been the 'absolute worst' writer she'd ever seen.

I took her encouragement and filed it away for later motivational use. She may be right and frankly I really don't care. Thanks to a very dear friend, I learned I had a unique voice that people began commenting on. I'd always been the cheerleader to other people.

Other than my dad and sports coaches, I never had a cheerleader as an adult – truly someone in my corner encouraging me. It was comforting and mildly concerning to hear praise as I was waiting for the shoe of rejection to fall. Sooner or later, they'd leave, die or find something else that entertained them more than me.

I also soaked up every positive word giving me hope and the courage to keep going! The funniest feedback I've received -to date was from my personal coach in Florida who calls me 'the southern-male version of yenta' – it's quite hilarious as I'm half-rag!

My writing began to take shape regarding cultures of work. When I look back on the tune-ups and turnarounds, I was a part of, the central theme was culture. I quickly learned the difference between climate and culture, and how the big shops bastardized and marketed the word culture.

I began testing the processes I'd previously used in every project – fine-tuning a methodology where it worked, where it didn't, why it didn't, evaluating circumstances, returning to clients and reformulating what we'd done previously.

I began to see patterns in companies, in people's behaviors and why it worked at some companies and not others. I'd offer to go back to the companies that fell off the rails and redux my work under an abridged program for free so they could see the benefit once the right people did the right thing at the right times for the right reasons. The acid test came when each company experienced lift in results and stronger relationships.

I knew I'd found something that could be replicated. And, the root cause of where the system broke down could always point to an issue with ego. I fought it for a handful of years, trying to get the three – ego, results and relationships – to be in balance, but they never did.

I see it all the time, people looking for, saying, posting, commenting, 'I want to get my life and work in balance.' I woke up in the middle of the night while traveling on the road and realized 'they' never balance, and they're not supposed to! There's always movement, shrinking, swelling, growing, reducing – there was a constant ebb and flow – a rhythm.

I could picture two images in my mind – a surfer riding a wave and the image of three circles. Concentric circles jumped off the page at me as I was studying to become an executive coach. Andrew Neitlich originated the image that kept appearing in my mind years earlier. My model takes it further. The space where the three meet is quite small, and THIS is what gives my model Voltage.

Voltage is force, pressure, tension; the difference in potential between two points and in my example three. But what IS voltage in this instance? What differentiates the model? What gives it it's energy? Here's where it gets interesting. As I began to write the 7-Steps book, I kept wrestling with the thought that something's just not meshing.

My rhythm is not in rhythm. I continued to write the book to get all the thoughts out of my head, off of my notebooks and onto paper. To tell what's next, we have to back track a little over a year. Business had flat-lined for some time after the crash in 2009 and I was desperately looking for avenues to diversify; to recapture what had been lost and find new revenue streams.

I was nearing a low point tired of the daily struggle to get back to where I wanted to be and frankly fed up. My daughter had invited me to 21 Days of Prayer in the summer of 2014.

I heard Chris Hodges, pastor of Church of the Highlands, throw out a challenge, 'give me a year and I guarantee your life will change.' I had nothing to lose and the conviction in his voice is what resonated with me. I need to know conviction! I was used to people telling me 'no', but what he said was an encouraging challenge, a yes...a been there, done that, T-shirt kind of challenge that I grabbed a hold of. It was a 'will you' just like Hilton had asked thirty-eight years earlier. I followed his guidance and wisdom and it was like flipping a light switch.

By this time, executive search was becoming more transactional, a commodity even, and I didn't want to compete in a race to the lowest cost. As we were forced to compete, we reduced our fees, increased our retainer and added onboarding and coaching services into the equation to recoup some of our fees. This field was foreign to most executives I'd previously met with and they struggled to make the connection. I began to communicate the model to hiring managers and C-suite we're offering a service 'like a business marriage counselor.'

It was standard practice for us to stay close to the hiring manager and our newly hired candidate throughout year one. We changed that model to include a communication system with both parties on a regular basis each month – onboarding.

Onboarding is creating a relationship so tight, a bond that couldn't be broken because the three of us had interwoven or interdependent interests in one another.

We created these Triads where we were all informed on what projects, milestone, deliverables, etc. must be met within certain timeframes. We all knew what was working, what wasn't, and I would coach both of them on our steps moving forward. During this period, I began studying to become an ICF Professional Certified Coach.

Business began to take off because we added great value to every relationship and each hire began adding value to their new company faster. We'd found a secret – hit our stride and began to take off. I give all the credit to that period in August of rededication of my life in the proper order and direction.

It was a no brainer for everyone involved because they could see the immediate impact and results. More companies were asking us to go deeper into their organization and fine-tune who and what was there. So, we did. We'd go into a search project and then cascade culture throughout a division or business unit.

The next three years were the best we'd ever had. I finally could catch my breath and feel I was making a difference...but was I really? I made a difference in the company's we served. I made a difference in the people who were hired, but it was still transactional.

More and more companies were learning to do more with less. I wanted 'them' to get the picture of 'do more with what you have'. It seemed the ones who weren't terminated at these companies were penalized for staying because they had to absorb the work from the ones who'd left.

I remembered the four-step process Chris used to onboard new members at Church of the Highlands and began researching his process. Here's the dichotomy – I dislike reading but I love to research. A bit of a problem, right? I also began reading more works from evangelical leaders on leadership to gain more knowledge and to see where there were parallels and intersections to the secular business world – what gap was present and what gap could be predicted.

If I can predict it, then I can prevent it and keep the cycle on track. The gap I uncovered was a pretty large chasm and it had always been there; that touchy subject, the elephant in the room no one wanted to address.

'You can't bring God into the office...it's just not done...' and other typical words were implied and some spoken. More reading, more researching and I came to the slippery slope conclusion we're living in as a society, and my takeaway was simple.

As 'one nation under God indivisible with Liberty and Justice for all' was fading away, we get things – life, government, business, religion, church, faith – out of order, things fall apart. I saw it, lived it, and researched from the great Roman Empire to today.

Time and time again, every business I worked with and every individual, team and work group, I worked with and led had one Achilles. It rarely varied and when they failed, it was for one reason – EGO! Male or female it didn't matter. If there was an ego at play, then eventually the system broke down.

I began studying the human mind as it relates to ego and many scientific works, psychology, biology, and anthropology. I also drew parallels to the evangelical leadership books and their interpretation of the same context. My process became a validated methodology in the field and in the classroom.

We all have moments in life where we 'get it' and then some where we miss it without even realizing we were 'in it.' This time was one of those moments.

The proverbial set of gears all clicked simultaneously - the four growth steps, four pillars, three concentric circles and my 'why' all harmoniously came together like pieces of a puzzle. I'd found where my personal and professional lives became interdependent upon one another, forever linked. Instead of running parallel for so long, the end of that third great business year, an interesting set of events occurred.

I would read, see or hear a number of key messages regarding Elegant Leadership with Voltage, and they began to increase in frequency. I was ready to go deeper in my own journey. I wasn't particularly aware at what cost, but I'm not one to back down from a challenge. Just tell me no! I'll show you!

CHAPTER 5

Are You Sure?

In just a few short months, everything I'd created - which was part of my problem - began to disappear, as if to say, 'you think you created this?' I'd had one of those conversations regarding commitment versus conviction with the Almighty. He asked, 'Are you sure, you're ready for this?' Couple things came immediately to mind. When the student is ready, the teacher will appear. And, the teacher is always quietest during a test.

Regardless of what it would do to me personally and financially, I knew I had to get my own house in order and rebuild in the proper order with the proper process. My mission was clear, my objective was easy to understand and simple to share.

What wasn't clear was coming to the understanding that a new journey was about to begin and obstacles to face as part of a new growth process. All I knew was that I wouldn't compromise what I'd originally set out to do - create or define a new model of leadership so no one would live through the rejection or abuse I'd lived through.

It struck me like a bolt of lightning one day - Voltage. It was so simple, so practical, and so powerful I couldn't believe I'd missed it earlier. We are made up of our habits. Our habits are made up of behaviors, perceptions, assumptions, beliefs, intentions and motives.

Our habits trigger who we are, what we believe, what gets done, and the things we do. When we work, we do stuff, stuff with our hands. We do stuff because of who we are or our being. What causes us to do stuff and to be who we are and what shapes these behaviors, habits and perceptions? Our head.

We think with our minds and our minds move us to act. Our minds also control and intercept our leadership through our ego favorably and unfavorably.

Many times, we lead from our head. And why not, that's how we were educated. It's easy for me to say and demonstrate the 40+ year old model is broken and unfortunately, so is how we are educated.

Our knowledge, skills, abilities and experiences tell us to do stuff. This reason alone is why we fail, fail often and fail greatly. What's missing? Our hearts. I didn't say our emotions; that's far different. We're not leading from a foundation of the heart.

We're leading with our head without any regard to our hearts or the impacts on other people. We're mainly dealing in facts and numbers instead of people, families, souls. Why do some relationships succeed, and others don't? Because we sacrifice people from our head. We think that's what we should do. Should is the one word, if I could, would be to eliminate from everyone's vocabulary. The word is based on probability.

Facts and numbers don't lie, but people do. When you put leadership in its proper order as Ken Blanchard writes, there's nothing that can stop you. To do the right thing at the right time for the right reason means to lead from your heart and your head will follow.

When those two are in alignment the hands naturally follow what the head has told it to do. When the hands are busy doing the right things your habits of being and doing are in the proper order. There is no ego involved. Why? Because our hearts are guiding us in order.

It's likely, you've heard and read countless gurus sell you, I mean tell you, they can transform you or they have a system that will transform how you work. To this day, I tell people, if anyone tries to tell you this - run, and run as fast and as far away as possible. They're selling some snake-oil vaporware. There is only one transformation and it's personal.

What I will say is the information in my life and my work creates motion. It gets you, your career and your organization to move forward. This is called transforMOTION. Big difference! I'm not transforming you.

You are allowing work to be done on you - your heart, head, hands and habits. There are at least ten verses I can point you to back up my statements. If you want to make significant change in your life, then you must first start with the one in the mirror and work from the inside-out. I'm not telling you anything you don't already know. But you must have the willingness and determination to follow through.

You know which door to walk through. You may not realize it, but you've been given another set of keys. All you are required to do is turn the damn key to open the door. This order also parallels what we found that worked in culture projects over the previous dozen years.

In order to 'fix' the culture, you're not fixing people, people will either fix themselves or they won't. You're putting the climate – the environment - in the proper order to allow people the space to recognize and understand internal, personal behavior changes are necessary. When an environment of safety exists, trust and cooperation emerge.

Now your people can do things and be things without fear of recrimination or retaliation. They can be innovative. Mistakes are methods of learning not markers of failure. Fail, fail often and fail faster; you're not a failure. Why? Safety originates from the heart.

When the environment is right, then leaders have earned the right to ask for the proper behaviors to be lived out. They've demonstrated how we're all expected to behave here. When the realization hit, it was like watching a firework's show. Every interaction, every relationship was either growing, building, repairing itself, because leaders were getting their act together.

When the environment is living its values through the current climate rhythm, the demonstrated behaviors improve productivity. It's never static and productivity is never on a continuum. It ebbs and flows like the surfer riding a wave.

As productivity becomes sustainable, then we've earned the right to produce the results we must have to be successful. By this time, I couldn't write fast enough to complete the final two steps in the book.

Let me quickly share with you what the seven steps are and what defines Voltage: a Blueprint – everyone needs a blueprint if they're going to build anything of value. Some can call it a roadmap, a dashboard or whatever.

The point is you need to find and work through a time-tested proven system in life that works personally and professionally. Being Comfortable in Your Own Skin is a huge deal for all of us and many of you aren't. We're trying to be someone we're not, trying to fit in somehow and struggling to embrace who we truly are and whose we truly are. The point is you cannot find freedom until you heal all of the wounds and embrace who you are. Stop fighting it!

You need a strategy. We call it an Elegant Strategy. Once you have a map, you need an implementation plan. With the first three pieces in order, you're going to find you were made uniquely and only you have certain knowledge, skills, and abilities. Only you have specific intangibles and a means to deliver them to be Clear, Concise and Compelling. We call this your edge.

The next step is all about relationships. Isn't life about having relationship, building community? As a society, our very survival is dependent on relationships. The missing piece about today's ever connected technological discoveries is we're becoming less and less dependent on one another and more dependent on tech. Without people forming relationships – teams, work groups, businesses, communities, etc., the tech discoveries aren't realized. Again, at what cost? We're everywhere and we're vital to every single success and failure on earth. Yet, we feel what's important to make life simpler by disconnecting from one another? We were made for community. Isolation and inactivity kill every relationship. Stop perpetuating the dissolution of people.

In this step, we expand practical advice to build community from one to many. I've said it countless times over and yet someone else who's wildly popular has assumed credit for this statement – your friends aren't on Facebook; you can't have a connection on LinkedIn, and you don't have a conversation on Twitter.

One of the last steps is we must move forward. In the military, you're taught to 'Get off the X' and in life we're told to never stand still – keep moving – motion is lotion.

Once you identify what your voice is and your unique gifts, you must move forward and do something with them. You're here for a reason. To have a relationship with our Creator, to heal from our brokenness so we can be built back up in His image.

We are to uncover or discover our unique selves and then to go out and make a difference in the lives of others. To do that, we must grow our problem-solving skills. There's a natural order of things; a logical sequence to who you are and everything you do.

In order, the seven steps along with the four pillars I shared earlier of heart, head, hands and habits ensure your ego is kept in check – you've wiped your feet at the door so to speak. The final piece is about those three concentric circles and how they intersect each other. You remember them, right?

Take a different viewpoint now and instead of thinking they intersect, think of the three circles as interdependent of one another. The small space in the middle that's been there the whole time is what's missing in your lead if it's not going so well. Some of you who are Rockstars already, holding space is what's been holding you back from moving forward. It's grace.

Even I didn't come to that conclusion until recently. Not that I'm some sage, but I had to experience my own discovery. I had to walk through the memories of my past, trying to go deeper to find the root cause of many a failure and success to come to the obvious conclusion. We can be so close to something that the image brushes past you without even realizing it or even living through it?

The conviction to my mission began to gain more speed, traction and velocity. Living in Alabama for over fifteen years, I've come to an appreciation of many unique and quirky things that are solely Alabama. Passion being one of them.

People in Alabama are passionate about football. They're also passionate about the movie, *Forrest Gump*. Tom Hanks famously said, "life is like a box of chocolates. You never know whatcha gonna get."

Profoundly accurate about our lives, we don't know what each day holds or if we'll see that next day. We do, however, have an assurance that He's with us and that all good comes from Him. In His fullness, we receive grace upon grace upon grace. Yet in the 'business world', we are quick to cull the herd, cut off the cancer and other clichés that make us sound as if we're Masters of the Universe. While in actuality, we were given that title by grace, we rose up the ranks by grace and it is only by grace we succeed.

Let's go back to my surfer analogy dude! One wave after another after another is how we draw divine fullness of grace. One wave being replaced by the next wave. Some of life's waves are favorable and some are not. You're not being punished because you did something bad when you were 12 or 47. We live on a failed planet that's not controlled by God. And the enemy will use any and every trick, trap and snare to get you to believe you're less than, you're a mistake, useless as a worn-out dish rag, that you should just end it because no one loves you, no one wants you. That was me! That was my life. Four dollars left and I had a choice to make. I like to think He helped me choose wisely.

We've all lived through some of our darkest of days and it's always darkest before the dawn. While tomorrow may be uncertain and not guaranteed, you can live one hour at a time. It's only sixty seconds long. There is no bottom to the well of grace at your disposal. Like the waves, they keep coming and coming, over and over without end. Once the box of chocolates is gone, it is gone and there is no more. We get what we don't deserve, and we don't get what we deserve. Thankfully, our life is not like a box of chocolates. We are loaded and reloaded every day with grace. It truly is the secret to great leadership – Elegant Leadership with Voltage.

I'm nowhere near the mountaintop today, nor am I in the valley. What I do know, is He is with me in the messy middle I find myself in. He reminds me how majestic the mountaintop view is and whispers to me, 'stay close.' I'm certainly not where I want to be in many of life's 'categories', and I'm comfortable in knowing who I am and whose I am.

I don't know about you, but I often hear in the back of my mind the cliché wisdom from my grandparents even to this day. 'You're either growing or you're rotting'. And, 'son, corn don't grow overnight. It's going to grow when it's damn good'n ready.'

I've always struggled with patience. I can only imagine how difficult it is for younger people with all the technology at their fingertips today. How they're not 100% impatient is beyond me. That brings me to social media.

I can tell you without a doubt I dislike having to be 'on it'. I find it shameless self-promotion, not unlike having to write this prequel. I've also learned a new perspective, too. People want to be encouraged by someone or something. It's part of the new community we're in – at a moment's notice, we're engaging people around the world.

I understand, in our disconnected yet always on society, these platforms are where people are most comfortable with each other. I find it both sad and disturbing. Sad, because we've lost touch with what relationship and community look and feel like.

Disturbing, because so many can hide in their 'command centers' behind a keyboard with monikers like 'warlock' and 'gingersnap' and positively or negatively affect a person's life via the medium of their choice.

Social media can be a platform for good, but it can also be a dangerous place, in my opinion. I feel forced to play the damn game. From where I sit, what was once hidden under a bushel basket, the message is shouted from the rooftops.

But, does it resonate with anyone? Does anyone care? My 'in the flesh' commentary is it seems to fall on deaf ears. Is that me or my ego talking? Both. Don't expect me to be anywhere near perfect. I'm not proselytizing here.

I'm trying to be a man after God's own heart in my own journey. I do, however, seek to find people who believe what I believe in – personally, professionally, emotionally, physically and spiritually. The verse from Matthew 10:27 was the impetus for *The Culture Whisperer*, the original blog I began in 2013.

It was and is the guiding theme I heard as a young boy walking through my own adventure oblivious as to how my life would unfold.

To this day, I have no idea how this story will evolve. I do know, however, my 'why' and what it will take to see it to fruition; so, I remain steadfast in my journey. What I don't know and have difficulty wrapping my arms around is when.

When will we see some measure of success? How long will I walk in this desert with the only solace being to trust Him? Is my own ego the motivator? Some of you will read this and say, it is. Some of you can see the space between the leaves and relate your own journey and wonder when, also.

We all have a choice to let go of it all, get out of it all once and for all. Don't miss the context here; it's my story I've opened up to you. I'm not looking to you for validation or for your opinion. You have your own story and your own journey to walk. I'm not selling anything here.

Don't misunderstand the purpose or the premise. I began writing the 7-Steps book in the summer of 2015 and within a year it was complete. The editing process took over two years to finish. My purpose for the book is not to hit the *NY Times Best Seller* list, hardly.

It was a measure of completing something I, again, was told I couldn't do. In my own OCD way, I struggled with getting every step perfect, every page perfect – visibly and audibly – and every thought connected to the next so the reader could understand the context and content in a clear, concise and compelling manner. I got it 'good enough' and then perfected it my way.

CHAPTER 6

You Have a Decision to Make

It's merely validation of a proven system and a megaphone for a new model of leadership in a simple, practical, powerful and graceful manner. What was once whispered to me and now shared across the rooftops of those who'll listen are the seven steps of Elegant Leadership.

The good side of social media helped me unite four principle thoughts with four hash tags, which seemingly appeared overnight. For whatever reason, those messages found their own order and logical sequence, too.

#DoSimpleBetter emerged long after Chicago Cubs Manager, Joe Maddon, coined the phrase for his World Championship baseball team. In leading people, teams and organizations, I've learned that sometimes the simplest answer is the best answer.

One of my goals in developing the ELV platform is to take what you do well and perfect it; to help you practice it until you can't get it wrong. The simplicity of it all is, well, *simple*.

#GoDeeper came from a client and friend who would challenge me on my faith, saying to take it further. Go deeper where you're uncomfortable, where the wounds are, where His grace will heal you if you allow it. #GoDeeper covers three thoughts – make room for Him when he wants you to be still, study something specific by being intentional and finally pray. Going deeper is *powerful*.

#AnAudienceOfOne was first developed by Athletes in Action during their camps decades ago. The intent was to help Christian athletes remember everywhere in life – even in a stadium full of people - "we live, move and have our being in Him," and it's His pleasure we should pursue above all else.

How different would our lives be if we played to an audience of one instead of our family, friends, peers and colleagues? Stop trying to prove our own worth to everyone else.

Please the one who made you and have your life attract others to Him as His opinion as the only one that matters...from the basket to the rooftop.

The book by David Cook, *Seven Days in Utopia*, and my personal experience visiting the sleepy village in the Texas Hill Country last year brought this message home as I struggle with 'when'. #AnAudienceOfOne is to seek His face, feel His touch and trust His presence. That advice is *practical*.

#EveryoneMatters is more than an inspirational model developed by Rob Chapman, author of the book and more than a one-day a year mantra. Elegant Leadership is about being authentic, taking your eyes off yourself, reaching back and lifting up. It's more than showing up as the leader, being the message with generosity and gratitude. We are to lead *gracefully* because everyone does matter.

My story is not fully written. Rather, it's a here's where we are along this journey. I'm convicted to helping people learn who and whose they are, to put their best self forward, to show up every day, lead with their gifts and the principle of doing the right thing at the right time for the right reason. It's not about raising the bar, moving the goal posts or moving the finish line further out towards frustration.

Your story is to leave a legacy regardless of what your journey has been thus far. If your gifts are encouraging, leading, speaking, writing, whatever exhortation they are, then lead by your own example. The five generations are here at this specific time for a reason. Isn't it time you found out what's your story that must be shared? What is your best next step?

- Commit to being intentional about the things you can do to move your organization and your career forward.

- Continue to improve your skills in your field or area of expertise.

- Act now to elevate the standard of You and those of your peers, colleagues and of your organization.

- Continue to grow, develop, learn and share your knowledge with others and develop another generation of leaders.

When we apply what we've learned, then it's not about outcomes! The question becomes, can you and will you follow the process? My story is about input. You've been controlled by your performance in life personally and professionally for too long. Neither you nor I can write our own epitaph. We don't have a say in how we'll be remembered, because those left behind will determine what's said.

I'm not a preacher nor a Bible 'thumper.' I believe there is a God and He has a plan for your life. Leadership is a lot like life - a series of choices, decisions and consequences. It's up to you to decide to invest the time to read and apply these principles or cast them aside. It's your choice and it's yours alone. Your choices have a direct impact on your destiny and the lives of others.

For many of us, we don't recognize the far-reaching effects of those small, everyday decisions, choices and consequences as a result. Your choices have a direct impact on your destiny and the lives of others. Maybe, the Elegant Leader journey is a calling for your life – a leap towards a life of significance – maybe it's not.

I hope my story is one you can relate to in a simple, powerful, practical and graceful way. We all have moments of fear for a variety of reasons regarding all kinds of decisions. You have a decision to make.

The question becomes, can you leave the fear of failure in its wake, regardless your decision? Do you have the courage to separate your identity from an outcome? Everyone has a story; everyone is on a journey and yours is no different.

How's your ego? Are you edging Him out or exalting Him only? Your life is one of significance – eternal influence impacting thousands and maybe millions of lives beyond your own legacy.

Now you know more of my story. Hopefully it encourages you to keep going. If you received value from it, feel free to pass it along to someone you know. They'll appreciate you sharing it.

About the Author

J. Scott Spector, native of Richmond, Virginia, is *The Culture Whisperer* - an executive with over 25 years of experience in change management, organizational development, and corporate turnarounds. He's worked with hundreds of executives, business professionals and athletes in over 12 countries.

He inspires leaders and businesses to inspire their people when they struggle with moving things forward in their organization, setting strategic direction, engaging and mobilizing employees, and creating a high-performance growth culture.

He received his MBA from the Pamplin School of Business at Virginia Polytechnic and State University in Blacksburg, Virginia. In 2017, he earned his Professional Coaching Certificate from the International Coaching Federation. He currently resides in Birmingham, Alabama, and has two grown children

Epilogue

Step in the Boat is the story behind the story. Several friends, peers and colleagues, who after reading my first work, *7 Steps to Become an Elegant Leader with Voltage*, suggested people may want to know the life and purpose behind that book. This work is my attempt to honor their wishes and feedback by offering a closer look inside while keeping as much privacy as possible. My hope is you will be encouraged in learning more of who I am, why I am the way I am and the motivating factors that drive my mission and purpose in life every day.

If you'd like to learn more about the 7 Steps to Become an Elegant Leader with Voltage, simply visit my website www.brookestoneassociates.com or amazon.com for a paperback version or to read an excerpt. A portion of the proceeds of each book purchase is given to the Red Circle Foundation, an immediate action foundation for Special Operators who've sacrificed their life for our freedom. For more about the foundation and their mission go to redcirclefoundation.org

Thank you for making time to learn more and for making a difference in the lives of others!